MOUNTAIN BIKING

Cecilia Minden-Cupp, Ph.D.
Reading Specialist

by K. C. Kelley

D1366875

Gareth Stevens Publishing
A WORLD ALMANAC EDUCATION GROUP COMPANY

Please visit our web site at: www.garethstevens.com
For a free color catalog describing Gareth Stevens Publishing's
list of high-quality books and multimedia programs,
call 1-800-542-2595 (USA) or 1-800-387-3178 (Canada).
Gareth Stevens Publishing's fax: (414) 332-3567.

Library of Congress Cataloging-in-Publication Data

Kelley, K. C.
    Mountain biking / by K. C. Kelley.
        p. cm. — (Extreme sports: an imagination library series)
    Summary: Briefly describes the equipment, techniques, various locations, and personalities
involved in riding mountain bikes.
    Includes bibliographical references and index.
    ISBN 0-8368-3723-1 (lib. bdg.)
    1. All terrain cycling—Juvenile literature. [1. All terrain cycling.] I. Title. II. Extreme
sports (Milwaukee, Wis.)
GV1056.K44   2003
796.6'3—dc21   2003042804

First published in 2004 by
Gareth Stevens Publishing
A World Almanac Education Group Company
330 West Olive Street, Suite 100
Milwaukee, WI 53212 USA

Text: K. C. Kelley
Cover design and page layout: Tammy Gruenewald
Series editor: Carol Ryback
Manuscript and photo research: Shoreline Publishing Group LLC

Photo credits: Cover © 2003 Greg Blasko, www.midwestphotos.com; p. 5 © Richard
Radstone/CORBIS; p. 7 © Chuck Savage/CORBIS; p. 9 © Sports Gallery/Al Messerschmidt;
pp. 11, 15 © AP/Wide World Photos; pp. 13, 17, 21 © Allsport; p. 19 © Duomo/CORBIS

Printed in the United States of America

1 2 3 4 5 6 7 8 9 07 06 05 04 03

Cover: John Laska competes in the Sport Class race at the
Alpine Valley Open in East Troy, Wisconsin. The Alpine
Valley Open is part of the Wisconsin Off-Road Series.

TABLE OF CONTENTS

Words that appear in the glossary are printed in **boldface**
type the first time they occur in the text.

HIT THE TRAIL!

Mountain bikes aren't just for the mountains! People ride mountain bikes on streets and dirt trails, through woods and fields, during all kinds of weather, and over any **terrain**.

A mountain bike can take you nearly anywhere your legs can pedal you. A mountain bike has a bulky **frame** and fat, nubby tires that grab the ground to handle many different riding conditions. You and your mountain bike can speed over a paved trail, slosh through mud, and skim across ice and snow. You can also enter mountain-biking races.

Read on for more fat-tire fun!

Mud? Water? Dirt? Bad weather? No problem — just strap on your helmet and head downhill. Mountain bikers love nasty conditions!

THE MOUNTAIN BIKE

Mountain bike frames are built tough to handle rough off-road trails. Many mountain bike models feature special springs or **shock absorbers**. These help cushion the impacts of bumps and stumps when you're trail riding.

Mountain bikes have as many as thirty **gears**. Shift gears to "power up" steep hills or gain extra speed on flat ground.

Gear shift levers are located either on the handlebars or within the handgrips. Just flip your thumbs or twist your wrists to change gears!

People of all ages enjoy mountain biking. Make sure to select a bike frame that fits your body size.

THE RIGHT EQUIPMENT

Always wear a helmet when mountain biking. Ask someone at a bike shop to help you find a helmet that fits your head properly.

Choose colorful biking clothing so that others can see you. Many riders also wear biking gloves and special padded shorts.

Bring water with you for the ride. You can also pack extra clothes, snacks, or energy bars in **panniers** (saddlebags) attached to your bike. Or you can wear a backpack.

Don't forget to pack a first-aid kit — and a spare inner tube!

On the trail, mountain bikers are dressed for comfort and safety. They carry water and spare parts for their bikes.

SIMPLE TRAILS

For your first mountain-bike ride, pick a simple trail near your house. Learn how to shift gears and use the brakes. Practice on familiar routes.

Always ride single file on a narrow or **single-track** (one-way) bike path. Ride on the right-hand side of a **double-track** (two-way) path. Let faster riders pass. When you need to pass someone, always pass to the left of the person riding in front of you.

Other trail-riding tips include the following:

- Dress for the weather.
- Don't be a litterbug.
- Respect the rights of others using the trail.

Trails can take you through green meadows or into deep forests. A responsible mountain biker respects the terrain he or she rides by staying on the path whenever possible and not littering.

GOIN' DOWNHILL

It's great fun to rattle down a mountain-biking trail. But if you hit a big tree root or a boulder, you might do an **"endo"** — and fly over your handlebars!

Recreational mountain bikers should begin on smaller hills. Focus on keeping your arms slightly bent and your pedals **parallel** to the ground as you go over rocks, bumps, and logs. When charging downhill, shift your weight back for better control.

Racing downhill on a mountain bike requires special skills. Extreme athletes who compete in the summer Olympic Games have coaches who help them perfect their riding techniques.

Going down while going downhill is one of the hazards of mountain biking. Downhill bikers learn to fall safely — or to avoid falling altogether!

MUD LOVERS

A cool thing about mountain bikes is getting dirty — on purpose! Many mountain bikers love to ride right after a rainstorm.

Riding in the mud can get tricky. If mud builds up along the wheel rims or brake pads, you might have trouble stopping. Practice shifting gears or dragging your feet instead of squeezing your brakes to stop. Make sure your tires are rugged and knobby to help you dig into the muck.

Always ride with others and stay on the trail. Don't forget to keep a clean towel in your backpack to clean up after your ride.

If this guy is the winner, imagine what the losers look like! Mountain bike racers know that the best place to go after the victory stand is to the showers.

READY, SET, GO!

Mountain bike racers compete in **cross-country** or downhill racing events.

Cross-country racers speed over a course that can be several miles long and include hills and valleys and can cut through mud or shallow water. At some places, riders must carry their bikes over tricky spots.

Downhill bikers race from the top of a mountain or high hill to the finish line at the bottom. Only a few riders make it all the way down the rutted, rocky course without falling.

But almost everyone who falls just gets up again!

And they're off! At the start of a cross-country race, each member in the huge pack hopes to move into the best position and take the lead.

ICE IS NICE

Winter is not an **obstacle** for a mountain bike. Thick, rugged tires crunch through the snow. Some snow mountain bikers use tires with metal studs that grip the ice.

Riding on packed snow can be as easy as riding on a dirt trail. Riding in powdery snow is harder and takes more energy.

Some ski areas set aside a slope or two just for winter mountain bikers. As an added bonus, snow helps cushion their falls!

Dress in layers when you ride in the snow. Wear an outer layer that is waterproof.

Winter is "snow" problem for this rider. She wears the proper clothing for her icy ride.

MOUNTAIN BIKE SUPERSTARS

Famous U.S. mountain bikers include Juli Furtado, Ned Overend, David "Tinker" Juarez, and Alison Dunlap. Mountain biking is very popular around the world, too. European riders won many medals at the 2000 Summer Olympics in Australia.

In the United States, the National Off-Road Bicycle Association (**NORBA**) sponsors races for all skills and age groups. Your local bike shop or the NORBA web site (www.usacycling.org/mtb) lists information on races in your area.

So strap on your helmet, pull on your gloves, and start pedaling that mountain bike!

World Champion mountain biker Brian Lopes speeds toward the finish line. Lopes holds the most NORBA victories of any U.S. mountain-biking racer.

MORE TO READ AND VIEW

Books (Nonfiction)   *Beginning Mountain Biking. Beginning Sports* (series).
    Julie Jensen (Lerner)
Extreme Mountain Biking. Extreme Sports (series).
    Arlene Bourgeois Molzahn (Capstone)
The Fantastic Book of Mountain Biking. Fantastic Book of (series).
    Brant Richards (Copper Beech)
Fundamental Mountain Biking. Fundamental Sports (series).
    Andy King (Lerner)
Mountain Biking. Action Sports Library (series). Bob Italia (ABDO)
Mountain Biking: Check It Out! Check It Out (series).
    Kristin Eck (Powerkids Press)
Pedal Power: How a Mountain Bike Is Made. David Hautzig (Lodestar)
Snow Mountain Biking. Extreme Sports (series).
    Jason Glaser (Capstone)

Books (Activity)   *Mountain Bikes: Maintaining, Repairing, and Upgrading.*
    Herman Seidl (Sterling)

Books (Fiction)   *Big Bad Beans. Cul-De-Sac Kids #22* (series). (Bethany House)
Marvin Redpost: Super Fast, Out of Control.
    Louis Sachar (Random House)
Mountain Bike Madness. Stepping Stone Books (series).
    Betsy Sachs (Random House)
Mountain Bike Mania. Matt Christopher (Little, Brown & Company)

Videos (Nonfiction)   *Ned Overend's Performance Mountain Biking.*
    John C. Davis (Director)

WEB SITES

Web sites change frequently, but we believe the following web sites are going to last. You can also use good search engines, such as **Yahooligans! (www.yahooligans.com)** or **Google (www.google.com)** to find more information about mountain biking. Some keywords that will help you are: *bicycling competitions, bike safety, fat tire, mountain biking,* and *Shimano Youth Series.*

bike.shimano.com/sponsorship/About.asp
The Shimano Youth Series site lists special competitions for younger riders, includes photos, and has a registration form you can download if you're interested in participating.

www.kidzworld.com/site/p1064.htm
KidzWorld has an interesting article on mountain biking star Mick Hannah and provides links to other articles that deal with extreme sports.

www.huntersville.org/police/traffic-kidszone.html
The Huntersville, North Carolina, Police Department offers important safety checks for bikers, examines myths about wearing a helmet, and offers a special safety quiz that deals with twelve common biking hazards.

www.mtnbikehalloffame.com/home.cfm
The *Mountain Bike Hall of Fame* includes short biographies of some of the athletes who excel in this extreme sport.

www.cheqfattire.com/
A popular midwestern fat tire festival includes a full weekend of bike rodeo activities for children. Get information regarding participation in parades, bicycle-decorating contests, a bike relay, log pull, obstacle course, and bicycle limbo. Prizes, surprises, and treats await young riders.

www.imba.com/sprockids/index.html
Visit the International Mountain Biking Association site for kids to find information about biking events, skills clinics, and races. Learn how to start your own mountain biking club for kids!

users.rcn.com/icebike/whybike.htm
For those who like it cold. Tips on winter riding and articles about those who do it.

www.imba.com/about/trail_rules.html
Read the International Mountain Bicycling Association's rules of the trail so you know what's expected of you and how to act.

GLOSSARY

You can find these words on the pages listed. Reading a word in a sentence helps you understand it even better.

cross-country — a ride that takes you some distance across meadows, up and down hills, or through forests. 16

double-track — (a bike path) wide enough to allow traffic in both directions or that lets two bikers ride side-by-side. 10

endo — flying over the handlebars and landing in front of your bike. 12

frame — the metal skeleton of a bike. 4, 6

gears — round metal disks of various sizes with teeth around the edge. 6, 10, 14

NORBA — National Off-Road Bicycle Association, an organization that sponsors mountain-biking races. 20

obstacle — anything that slows or stops your movement or activity. 18

panniers — also called saddlebags, are the bags or containers strapped to each side of a bike's rear wheels. 8

parallel — alongside of but not touching. 12

recreational — an activity done just for fun or exercise instead of competition. 12

shock absorbers — springs under the seat or attached to the front wheel of a bike that help cushion the ride. 6

single-track — (a one-way trail) usually just wide enough for one bike. 10

terrain — landscape. 4

INDEX